Seal or Sea Lion

Which Is Which?

By Tamra B. Orr

Published in the United States of America by
Cherry Lake Publishing
Ann Arbor, Michigan
www.cherrylakepublishing.com

Reading Adviser: Marla Conn, MS, Ed., Literacy specialist, Read-Ability, Inc.
Content Adviser: Susan Heinrichs Gray

Photo Credits: ©Alan De Witt/Shutterstock, cover (left); ©Foto 4440/Shutterstock, cover (right); ©Joost van Uffelen/Shutterstock, 4; ©Dolores Harvey/Shutterstock, 6; ©Lisa Beeby/Shutterstock, 8; ©Rusty Dodson/Shutterstock, 10; ©Serova_Ekaterina/Shutterstock, 12; ©Ondrej Prosicky/Shutterstock, 14; ©Kichigin/Shutterstock, 16; ©Longjourneys/Shutterstock, 18; ©Enrique Aguirre/Shutterstock, 20

Library of Congress Cataloging-in-Publication Data

Names: Orr, Tamra, author.
Title: Seal or sea lion / Tamra B. Orr.
Description: Ann Arbor : Cherry Lake Publishing, [2019] | Series: Which is which? | Includes bibliographical references and index. | Audience: K to Grade 3.
Identifiers: LCCN 2019005989 | ISBN 9781534147355 (hardcover) | ISBN 9781534150218 (paperback) | ISBN 9781534148789 (pdf) | ISBN 9781534151642 (hosted ebook)
Subjects: LCSH: Seals (Animals)—Juvenile literature. | Sea lions—Juvenile literature.
Classification: LCC QL737.P64 O77 2019 | DDC 599.79—dc23
LC record available at https://lccn.loc.gov/2019005989

Cherry Lake Publishing would like to acknowledge the work of the Partnership for 21st Century Skills.
Please visit *www.p21.org* for more information.

Printed in the United States of America
Corporate Graphics

CONTENTS

Sea lions tend to be more social than seals.

Fin-Footed

Seals and sea lions are often mistaken for one another. Even their names are **similar**! But look closer. Can you spot the differences? Can you tell which is which?

While these animals are different, they have a lot in common. Both are *pinnipeds*, which is a Latin word for “fin-footed.” They use those fins or flippers on land and in water. These creatures are found almost

Seals, like this one pictured, can't rotate their back flippers, but sea lions can.

everywhere in the world. The only other pinniped is the walrus.

Like many **mammals**, seals and sea lions have **sensitive** whiskers. These water animals use their whiskers as guides. The two creatures have another thing in common: **blubber**, or fat. They have thick layers of blubber under their skin. This acts like a big coat. It keeps them warm in the cold water.

These sea creatures differ in size, though. The California sea lion is the one you see doing tricks at SeaWorld. It is smaller than most seals. These flippered mammals weigh

Some sea lions can sleep completely underwater.

between 250 and 750 pounds (113 and 340 kilograms). The largest sea lion is the Steller sea lion. It weighs between 800 and 2,500 pounds (363 and 1134 kg).

Seals vary greatly in size. The smallest type of seal is about 110 to 150 pounds (50 to 68 kg). The largest type of seal can weigh between 2,000 and 8,500 pounds (907 and 3,855 kg)!

Look!

Have you ever seen a sea lion balance a ball on its nose? It actually uses its whiskers to keep the ball in place. It has 76 whiskers, 38 on each side! They are controlled by muscles. The whiskers can be moved in different directions much like humans use their hands.

Sea lions don't chew their food. They swallow it whole.

Wiggle and Walk

Both seals and sea lions have four flippers. But they are very different. Seals' flippers are smaller in front. They are stubby, furry, and have small claws on each end. Seals' back flippers angle backward. They help seals move quickly and smoothly through the water. On land, however, seals aren't all that graceful. They have to wiggle on their bellies to move across the ground. Because of this, seals tend to only come on land at certain times. They do this when it

Sea lions' ability to move so well on land means they are often used in marine shows, like SeaWorld.

is time to find a **mate**, give birth, or escape hungry **predators**.

Sea lions' flippers are long, large, and covered in skin. Their back flippers can turn, or rotate. They use their flippers to steer and push through the water. They also use them on land to "sit up" and to walk across the ground. They spend a lot more time on land than seals. They can even chase **prey** over short distances.

Ask Questions!

Both sea lions and seals are carnivores. That means they eat meat. Sea lions like to eat squid, octopus, birds, and fish. Seals like to eat birds and fish too. But they also snack on harder foods like **crustaceans** and **mollusks**. Look up examples of crustaceans and mollusks. Why do you think sea lions don't eat these types of food?

Seals and sea lions can stay underwater for long periods of time.
But they need to breathe air just like us!

Dive and Swim

Sea lions and seals eat food that mainly comes from the water. So these sea creatures spend a lot of time hunting underwater. Seals and sea lions share another skill. They can dive deep under the water and stay there for a long time. Sea lions can dive up to 900 feet (274 meters) deep and stay there for up to a half hour. They consume about 10 to 18 pounds (4 to 8 kg) of food a day.

Elephant seals can dive deeper than 4,900 feet (1,500 m) and stay underwater

When seals dive underwater, their heart rate slows down. This helps them stay underwater without air for longer periods of time.

for up to 2 hours. These large sea creatures can also eat up to 50 pounds (23 kg) of food a day!

There's another way to tell the difference between sea lions and seals. Notice how many of them you see. Sea lions gather in groups called herds or rafts. There are sometimes as many as 1,500 in a herd at one time. Seals are just the opposite. These creatures aren't very social. They tend to be alone most of the time.

Make a Guess!

How are seals able to stay under the water for so long? One reason is because they can slow down their heartbeat. How would this help them use less oxygen?

Sea lions can swim up to 25 miles (40 kilometers) per hour.

Grunts and Barks

There are two more clues for recognizing sea lions and seals. Both of them involve ears!

First, use your ears. Do you only hear a soft snuffle or a grunt? Then chances are you are seeing a seal. It is a fairly quiet animal and rarely makes any sound at all. Do you hear some very noisy barking and honking? If so, it is a sea lion. The barking might even turn into a nasty roar! Then you are hearing two

Seals can only reach speeds of up to 18 miles (28 km) per hour.

male sea lions trying to scare each other away from the females.

Second, look at their ears. If you see ears, it is a sea lion. If you only see holes where the ears should be, it is a seal. Even though seals do not have outside ears, they hear just fine!

They are two of the ocean's most amazing creatures. Each one is special, so learn the difference!

Think!

One of the greatest dangers to sea animals is trash in the ocean. Items like fishing nets often hurt the animals. What could be done to help them?

GLOSSARY

blubber (BLUHB-ur) thick layer of fat

crustaceans (kruh-STAY-shuhnz) hard-shelled animals

mammals (MAM-uhlz) animals that feed milk to their young and usually have hair or fur covering most of their body

mate (MATE) another animal to produce babies with

mollusks (MAH-luhsks) animals that live mostly in water and have a soft body usually enclosed in a hard shell

predators (PRED-uh-turz) animals that live by hunting other animals for food

prey (PRAY) an animal that is hunted or killed by another animal for food

sensitive (SEN-sih-tiv) affected by even slight changes

similar (SIM-uh-lur) nearly but not exactly alike

FIND OUT MORE

BOOKS

Kirkwood, Roger, and Simon Goldsworthy. *Fur Seals and Sea Lions.* Melbourne: CSIRO Publishing, 2013.

Marcos, Victoria. *My Favorite Animal: Sea Lions.* Irvine, CA: Xist Publishing, 2018.

Rockwood, Leigh. *A Seal and a Sea Lion.* New York, NY: PowerKids Press, 2013.

Ryndak, Rob. *Seal or Sea Lion?* New York, NY: Gareth Stevens Publishing, 2016.

WEBSITES

National Geographic Kids—California Sea Lion
https://kids.nationalgeographic.com/animals/california-sea-lion/#sea-lion-rock.jpg
Learn more about the California sea lion.

YouTube—How Are Seals Different from Sea Lions?
https://www.youtube.com/watch?v=Cv_Yss8qPLg
Discover more fascinating differences between seals and sea lions from the Smithsonian's YouTube channel.

INDEX

ABOUT THE AUTHOR

Tamra Orr is the author of hundreds of books for readers of all ages. She graduated from Ball State University, but moved with her husband and four children to Oregon in 2001. She is a full-time author, and when she isn't researching and writing, she writes letters to friends all over the world. Orr enjoys life in the big city of Portland, and has taken many trips to nearby Seattle to watch—and listen—to the sea lions on the pier.